ECONOMIC ISSUES 28

Moral Hazard

Does IMF Financing Encourage Imprudence by Borrowers and Lenders?

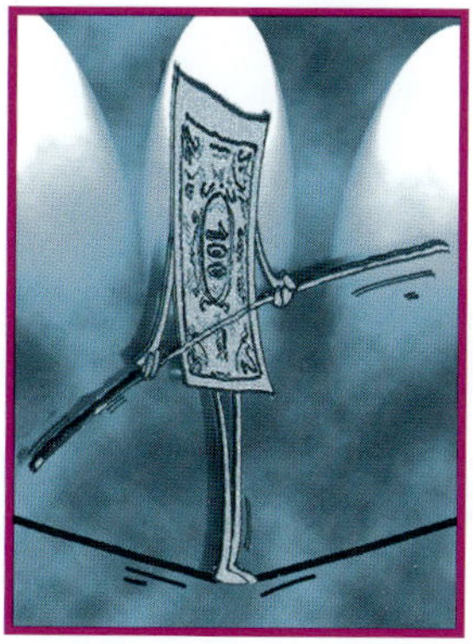

Timothy Lane
Steven Phillips

INTERNATIONAL MONETARY FUND
WASHINGTON, D.C.

Series Editor
Jeremy Clift
IMF External Relations Department

Cover design and composition
Massoud Etemadi, Jack Federici, and
the IMF Graphics Section

ISBN 1-58906-088-1
ISSN 1020-5098

Published March 2002

To order IMF publications, please contact:

International Monetary Fund, Publication Services
700 19th Street, N.W., Washington, D.C. 20431, U.S.A.
Tel: (202) 623-7430 Telefax: (202) 623-7201
E-mail: publications@imf.org
Internet: http://www.imf.org

Preface

The Economic Issues series aims to make available to a broad readership of nonspecialists some of the economic research being produced on topical issues by IMF staff. The series draws mainly from IMF Working Papers, which are technical papers produced by IMF staff members and visiting scholars, as well as from policy-related research papers.

This Economic Issue is based on IMF Working Paper WP/00/168, *Does IMF Financing Result in Moral Hazard?,* October 2000. Citations for the studies reviewed are provided in the original paper which readers can purchase ($10.00) from the IMF Publication Services, or download from *www.imf.org*. Jacqueline Irving prepared the text for this pamphlet.

"Moral hazard remains a concern. Private institutions may be encouraged to lend and invest recklessly—or at least more than they should—by the belief that the Fund will ensure that their creditors can repay them."

Anne Krueger, First Deputy Managing Director,
International Monetary Fund,
in an address to the National Economists' Club,
American Enterprise Institute, Washington, D.C.
November 2001

Does IMF Financing Produce Moral Hazard?

Moral hazard is a term often used when analyzing the effects of insurance. It refers to the idea that the very provision of insurance raises the likelihood of the event being insured against taking place. This is because insurance reduces the incentives for the insured party to take preventive actions. Some simple examples would be:

- A homeowner taking less care in locking up his home once it is insured;
- A motor vehicle owner driving more recklessly because his vehicle is insured;
- A person taking less care of his health once he has health insurance.

In the financial context, economists and policy makers debate whether the availability of financial support from institutions like the International Monetary Fund (IMF) leads to moral hazard. That is, does the IMF's role as a lender to countries in financial crisis actually encourage borrowers and lenders to behave in ways that makes a crisis more likely?

Following the series of financial market crises that beset emerging markets in the past several years, some analysts have suggested that IMF financial support *does* give rise in some cases to reckless lending by banks and other financial institutions. These institutions are believed to lend without adequate regard to risk because they are confident that countries in difficulty can draw on IMF support if things go wrong. At the same time, it is argued that when countries know they can turn to the IMF in the event of a crisis, this dulls their motivation to take timely action to prevent a crisis. Concerns about moral hazard have had a prominent place in recent discussions on how the architecture of the international financial system should be reformed and what the IMF's role should be.

To the extent that IMF financing helps contain the total economic damage induced by a crisis, the availability of this financing could well encourage both borrowers and lenders to take some risks that they would not otherwise take. But this is not necessarily a problem: on the contrary, one of the IMF's stated purposes is "to give confidence to members by making the general resources of the IMF temporarily available to them under adequate safeguards." Rather, the important questions are whether IMF support encourages borrowers and lenders to take *excessive* or *imprudent* risks and whether these extra risks outweigh the benefit of IMF financial help in easing the impact of the crisis. One such benefit is that, in a liquidity crisis, IMF financing may help compensate for the collective-action problem associated with creditors' self-defeating race to the exits. Answers to these questions turn on another key question: How important is any moral hazard created by the IMF in influencing borrowers' and lenders' behavior before a crisis?

Despite the prominence of moral hazard in policy discussions, there has been little research to examine its empirical relevance until recently. This pamphlet looks at some preliminary evidence in considering the degree of moral hazard associated with IMF financial support.

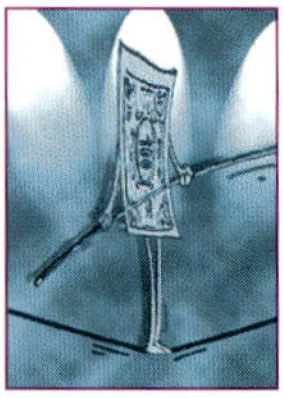

Understanding Moral Hazard

First, how could moral hazard arise in connection with the IMF's financial support? Moral hazard is a forward-looking concept: where moral hazard exists in financial markets, borrowers and lenders take risks *now* based on the support they anticipate receiving in the future if certain undesirable events occur.

Looking specifically at the prospect of moral hazard resulting from IMF financing, it bears emphasizing that the IMF's support does not take the form of a simple cash payout (such as an insurer would make). Rather, IMF support comes as a loan to be repaid with interest. So the amount of "insurance benefit" in the case of IMF financing is the difference between the rate at which a country could otherwise borrow (which may be very high during a crisis) and the IMF's lending rate (which is tied to market interest rates in industrial countries).

Creditor-side moral hazard—which can take the form of a greater willingness to lend—can be distinguished from moral hazard of the debtor, or borrowing country—manifested as reduced motivation to take preventive action. The availability of financial support from the IMF could entail either debtor-side or creditor-side moral hazard—or both—to the extent that this support could affect outcomes for debtors, creditors, or both.

One problem in trying to find out whether IMF financing leads to moral hazard is the difficulty of knowing what would have happened without the rescue package. In the absence of the IMF, a country facing financing difficulties would have to try alternatives, possibly including but not limited to default on foreign debt. For example, a country might allow its currency to depreciate further, making its exports more competitive and allowing itself to inflate away more of its domestic-currency debt. The alternative that would in fact be chosen determines how the availability of financing under an IMF-supported program affects the relative returns on different types of debt.

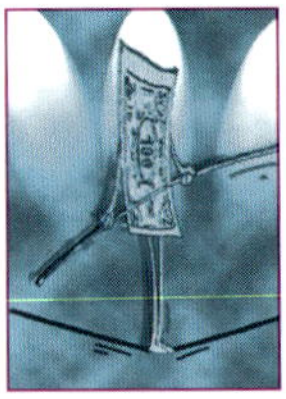

Are Creditors Confident the IMF Will Save Them?

A look at interest rate data and spreads—which can provide measures of perceived risk—can quickly dismiss one extreme view about the moral hazard facing investors. The spread between the yield on bonds with default risk and the yield on default-free bonds (such as U.S. Treasury bonds) shows how much additional interest investors must earn in order to hold a riskier bond and thus reflects both changes in investor perceptions about risk and changes in the creditworthiness of creditors. The higher the default risk of a particular country's debt issue, the wider the spread between yields on the particular debt issue and yields on U.S. Treasury bonds with similar maturities. If private creditors truly believed that the IMF completely guarantees the debt service of its member countries, this would mean that all such members—or at least those deemed "too big to fail"—would face the same interest rate in a common currency. Of course, this is not the case: in reality, different countries encounter a wide range of interest rates on their U.S. dollar borrowing. See, for example, Figure 1, which shows interest rate spreads (expressed in basis points, that is one-hundredths of a percentage point) for a sample of 21 emerging market countries at the end of 1998. Indeed, Russia and Brazil—though they might be considered too big to fail—have some of the widest interest rate spreads.

Any perception of a "complete guarantee" also can be proved false by the tendency of spreads to increase during a crisis. Even the fact that crises happen at all provides further proof that market participants do not see IMF financing as eliminating risk. Evidently, the

Figure1.
Yield spreads on dollar-denominated debt
(In basis points; as of December 31, 1998)

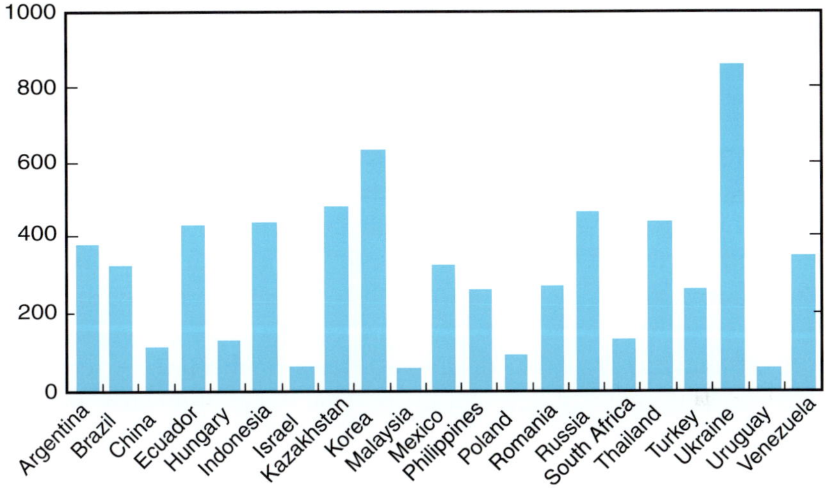

Source: Bloomberg.
Note: Yield spreads are calculated by comparing domestic U.S. dollar–denominated debt with U.S. treasury bonds maturing on similar dates.

markets see IMF and other official support as limited and/or dependent on uncertain developments. At the same time, of course, this does not prove the extreme opposite view—that an IMF-supported program has absolutely no influence on creditors' prospects of repayment.

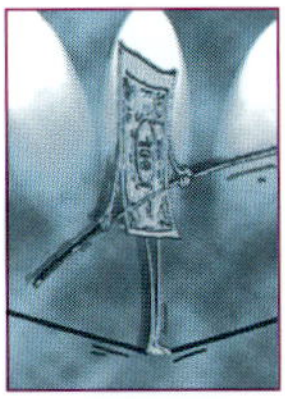

Does the "News" Reveal Moral Hazard?

A "news-based" or "event study" approach can also be used to explore the moral hazard question. In this approach, one would first identify specific events that might have relayed new information to markets that would influence their outlook for the future availability of IMF financial support. By using daily data and looking at the behavior of spreads over very short periods, this approach seeks to isolate the influence of the IMF-related news from other factors. *If* investors do believe that the availability of IMF financing significantly influences the riskiness of their investments, secondary market bond prices can be expected to react immediately to such news.

Of course, this type of approach has its limitations—particularly that it cannot distinguish moral hazard (undesirable effects on economic behavior) from the desirable effects of the IMF in reducing the real economic damage of a crisis. This stacks the cards in favor of finding evidence consistent with moral hazard. On the other hand, it is also possible that some of the events identified are not entirely "news," as markets may have anticipated these events beforehand; this would weaken the power to detect moral hazard.

In any case, the event study approach essentially looks for *changes* in the degree—rather than the presence—of IMF-induced moral hazard. This makes the approach especially well suited to exploring the question of whether changes in policies affecting IMF lending during the 1990s have produced an increase in moral hazard.

Let's first look at "events" in the 1990s that took the form of announcements of new IMF-supported programs at the beginning of financial crises. The case of Mexico in late 1994 to early 1995 is of particular interest since it has been described as setting an important precedent and even contributing directly to the Asian crisis a few years later. The Stand-By credit for Mexico approved in February 1995 was for US$17.8 billion—the largest ever approved for any member country up until that point, both in absolute amount and in relation to the member's IMF quota.

Did the scale—or other aspects of the design—of the IMF-supported program for Mexico change creditors' expectations about how they would fare in future crises? Data from the period shows that interest rate spreads rose sharply from late December 1994. Subsequent announcements of new IMF-supported programs in early 1995 did not prevent further increases—let alone quickly return spreads to their precrisis levels. So, applying an events-based approach in this case does not reveal moral hazard.

Notably, events in Mexico in 1994–95 did not seem to influence spreads on bonds of several Asian emerging markets: spreads did not widen when Mexico began to run into financial difficulties and they did not narrow when IMF support for Mexico was approved—nor did they narrow when the announcements were made preceding approval. This suggests that most investors did not see the Mexican program as having much relevance to the creditworthiness of the Asian newly industrializing countries.

Next, let's look at whether the IMF's approval—and six associated announcements—of large financial arrangements with Thailand, Indonesia, and Korea in 1997 produced moral hazard. The IMF authorized drawings of up to US$3.9 billion, US$10.1 billion, and US$21 billion, respectively.

But spreads did not change significantly in response to the first three announcements, which were made before the onset of a more general crisis in October 1997. The J.P. Morgan Emerging Markets Bond Index (EMBI) spreads increased somewhat following the fourth announcement—the opposite of what would be expected in the presence of moral hazard. While spread declines accompanied the last two announcements (both related to Korea), these declines seem too small to be meaningful. So, here, as well, the evidence fails to support the idea that the IMF's involvement (in this case, in Asia) gave fresh reassurance to investors in emerging markets in general.

Another possible indication of moral hazard would be the reaction of financial markets to changes in the IMF's access limits—ceilings on the amount that the IMF will lend to a country, barring exceptional circumstances. A ceiling is set on both the financing committed in a given year and cumulatively; both are expressed as a percentage of the country's IMF quota. In principle, raising the IMF's access limits might increase moral hazard *if* markets were to link this with a sign of the IMF's openness to lending in larger amounts. If we look at the market response to an increase in the annual access limits in October 1994 (from 68 percent to 100 percent of a member's quota), we see no sign of increased moral hazard: spreads did not narrow.

Now, let's consider how markets react to changes in the size of the IMF's total resources. When IMF press releases in September and December 1997 and again in February 1998 relayed the news that the IMF would seek an increase in its members' quotas—a decision that should have increased the perceived likelihood of an expansion of IMF resources—emerging market spreads did not decline in any significant way. Indeed, spreads *increased* by a sizable amount after the final announcement in January 1999 that the quota increase had occurred.

Still, caution must be used in interpreting the markets' response above as refuting the notion of IMF-induced moral hazard. These market responses might also mean that investors had largely anticipated the quota increase.

Looking more closely at the response to an event that more clearly represented news to markets can be useful. Within the overall process of the quota increase, securing the approval of the United States, the IMF's largest shareholder, was arguably the highest hurdle to cross, given that congressional support initially seemed to be lacking. So, with this in mind, the U.S. legislature's assent to the full request in October 1998 may have been the most newsworthy event in the process. And, since this approval came at a time when the IMF's liquidity position had become unusually weak, markets may have viewed the approval as pushing back a constraint on future IMF lending that had threatened to become binding in the near future. This event in fact was associated with a substantial decline in spreads—which seems consistent with the notion that the potential availability of IMF financing brings about some degree of moral hazard.

But a note of caution is called for before drawing this conclusion: the evidence is not very solid, after all, because the observed fall in spreads was not unusually large compared with typical short-term movements. Here, there is a problem caused partly by the way the news of U.S. approval was relayed—gradually, with hints of impending approval in the weeks before it actually happened, rather than as a single, abrupt announcement. This could indicate the need for a longer "window" to pick up the full impact of the news. But with a longer window, it becomes harder to separate the effect of the quota increase from that of other simultaneous events—especially the U.S. Federal Reserve's surprise interest rate cut, announced on October 15.

All the events discussed above had the potential to signal to markets that the IMF's lending policies were becoming more liberal—thereby potentially providing greater assurance to investors. But, with one exception, these events were not associated with a substantial narrowing of emerging market yield spreads (see Figure 2).

Figure 2.
Yield spreads, October 1994–March 1999

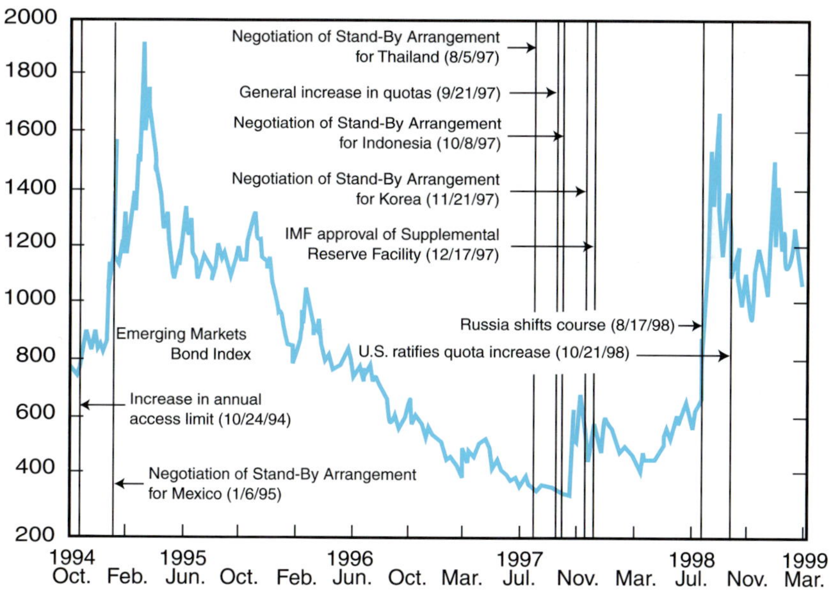

Source: J.P. Morgan.

Rounding out the analysis, Russia's devaluation and effective partial default on domestic government debt in August 1998 might have sent a worrying signal to investors. While there were signs of trouble in Russia before August, there can be little doubt that the Russian default was news to the market. Indeed, before the Russian crisis, some investors spoke glibly of a "moral hazard play," designed to exploit the perception of Russia as "too big too fail." Some observers actually pointed to the IMF's release of a credit to Russia and its approval of a further lending increase in June and July 1998 as proof of Russia's too-big-to-fail standing. But the events of August 1998 snuffed out any expectation that further IMF credits would flow as needed to keep Russia afloat.

In this case, the "news" was not any particular IMF action but, rather, the realization of the *absence* of IMF action that might have allowed Russia to avoid the measures announced on August 17, as well as the subsequent absence of any quick scramble on the part of the IMF to inject new financing.

In fact, while announcements during the two months ahead of the default, concerning the IMF and Russia, did not seem to influence bond markets, spreads generally widened dramatically around the time of Russia's August 17 announcement. This was the case especially during the days immediately following. Of course, the widening of the Russian bond spread itself accounted for part of the Emerging Market Bond Index spread jump, but the large widening of spreads was general.

One way to interpret this is to conclude that the lack of new support from the IMF and other official sources to Russia in August 1998 held an unsettling lesson for bond markets—thereby *reducing* moral hazard. This, in turn, would imply that some degree of IMF-induced moral hazard had existed in the first place. But some part of the widening of bond spreads outside Russia may have been due, at least partly, to contagion (through various channels)—or to a "wake-up" call that this event sent to investors about the riskiness of sovereign debt, rather than to any specific decline of moral hazard associated with the IMF.

What can we conclude from the review of these cases? Certainly, we can rule out the most extreme form of moral hazard—whereby investors believe they have a full IMF guarantee—even for the "too-big-to-fail" countries. Evidence on the extent of moral hazard is less clear cut. But a check of some key implications of the moral hazard story against the data fails to produce a smoking gun. Notably, there is no proof of the notion that IMF actions since the Mexican crisis have brought on a new era of much greater moral hazard.

At the same time, these results must be recognized as preliminary. The event study approach has obvious limitations because of the difficulty of disentangling the effects of the events in question from those of other circumstances. Moreover, news that could have caused a perception that IMF financing was more readily available may have made emerging market countries more willing to borrow. If this were the case—and if the resulting effects on interest rate spreads were immediate—this could have offset the impact of creditors' greater willingness to lend, making moral hazard hard to detect. This possibility may need to be explored by examining the quantities of financing provided to emerging markets as well as the interest rate spreads.

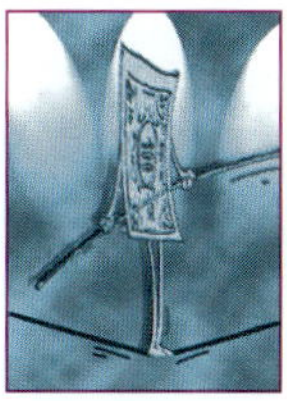

Does the Scale of IMF Lending Create Serious Moral Hazard?

Why might investors not see the IMF as guaranteeing their investments? This may be for either or both of two reasons: they may be uncertain of whether IMF financial help will arrive or they may doubt the ability of such help to protect their positions. What about the *scale* of the IMF's financial support? Was the financing able to cover a substantial portion of their exposures (assuming that all this support was used for that purpose)?

In forecasting the likely amount of future IMF support, private investors might note the IMF's formal limits on a member's access to its resources. These limits are related to the quota (or capital) subscriptions that member countries pay.

A look at the record of IMF support, however, suggests these limits alone may not be enough to gauge expectations. In most IMF-supported programs, the amount actually accessed is well below the ceiling allowed. But, in some exceptional cases—indeed, the cases that have attracted recent controversy—approved access can go well beyond these limits. And, in certain cases, the IMF has also put together support packages from other official sources, going well beyond its own financing.

In the large majority of Stand-By and Extended Arrangements, annualized access to IMF resources tends to be small: for example, in 1997, most Stand-By Arrangements had access in the range of ½ to 1 percent of the member's GDP. Considering typical ratios of external debt to GDP, it is hard to see how access on this scale could lead private creditors to believe that the IMF guarantees their investments. The same conclusion holds even when one considers exceptionally large access to IMF resources.

Other factors limit the assurance to investors provided by IMF-supported financing packages. The published numbers refer to initial commitments and investors cannot take full disbursement of these amounts as a given: IMF and other official support is generally phased over time and depends on the particular program remaining on track. In some cases, bilateral financing has not materialized as originally announced. Thus, even in exceptional cases, the IMF's support is not on a sufficient scale to fully bail out private investors—and the picture does not change significantly with the inclusion of other official funds mobilized.

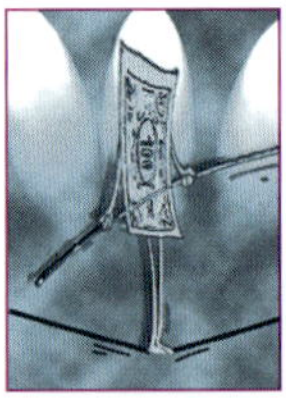

Conclusions

The argument that IMF financing creates moral hazard cannot be lightly dismissed. From the outset, this pamphlet recognizes that, to the extent IMF-supported programs try to contain the total economic costs of financial crises, some element of moral hazard—a greater willingness of creditors and debtors to take risks of such crises—is, in principle, an unavoidable consequence. But the key question, rather than a matter of presence or absence, is the *degree* of moral hazard. The most basic evidence, even in the case of countries that are supposed to be too big to fail, refutes the most extreme hypothesis—that investors believe they have a full guarantee from the IMF in the event of a financial crisis.

Beyond this, this pamphlet has drawn on a number of recent cases of financial market crises in emerging markets to show that moral hazard's role may have been seriously overstated by some observers. This, of course, does not negate the need to consider the implications of moral hazard in assessing possible reforms to the international financial system. Even if moral hazard is not empirically important, it could become so if these arrangements or market mechanisms were to change. Moreover, the results do not minimize the need for sensible steps to prevent IMF financing from serving primarily to bail out private creditors, such as recent efforts to secure greater private sector involvement in addressing financial crises. But such policies should not be guided by an unsubstantiated belief that moral hazard is an overwhelming problem. As long as further evidence is needed to establish the magnitude of moral hazard, such action should proceed cautiously, weighing the possibility of moral hazard against other implications of the availability of IMF financing in alleviating the effects of crises.

The Economic Issues Series

1. *Growth in East Asia: What We Can and What We Cannot Infer.* Michael Sarel. 1996.
2. *Does the Exchange Rate Regime Matter for Inflation and Growth?* Atish R. Ghosh, Anne-Marie Gulde, Jonathan D. Ostry, and Holger Wolf. 1996.
3. *Confronting Budget Deficits.* 1996.
4. *Fiscal Reforms That Work.* C. John McDermott and Robert F. Wescott. 1996.
5. *Transformations to Open Market Operations: Developing Economies and Emerging Markets.* Stephen H. Axilrod. 1996.
6. *Why Worry About Corruption?* Paolo Mauro. 1997.
7. *Sterilizing Capital Inflows.* Jang-Yung Lee. 1997.
8. *Why Is China Growing So Fast?* Zuliu Hu and Mohsin S. Khan. 1997.
9. *Protecting Bank Deposits.* Gillian G. Garcia. 1997.
10. *Deindustrialization—Its Causes and Implications.* Robert Rowthorn and Ramana Ramaswamy. 1997.
11. *Does Globalization Lower Wages and Export Jobs?* Matthew J. Slaughter and Phillip Swagel. 1997.
12. *Roads to Nowhere: How Corruption in Public Investment Hurts Growth.* Vito Tanzi and Hamid Davoodi. 1998.
13. *Fixed or Flexible? Getting the Exchange Rate Right in the 1990s.* Francesco Caramazza and Jahangir Aziz. 1998.
14. *Lessons from Systemic Bank Restructuring.* Claudia Dziobek and Ceyla Pazarbaşıoğlu. 1998.
15. *Inflation Targeting as a Framework for Monetary Policy.* Guy Debelle, Paul Masson, Miguel Savastano, and Sunil Sharma. 1998.
16. *Should Equity Be a Goal of Economic Policy?* IMF Fiscal Affairs Department. 1998.

17. *Liberalizing Capital Movements: Some Analytical Issues.* Barry Eichengreen, Michael Mussa, Giovanni Dell'Ariccia, Enrica Detragiache, Gian Maria Milesi-Ferretti, and Andrew Tweedie. 1999.

18. *Privatization in Transition Countries: Lessons of the First Decade.* Oleh Havrylyshyn and Donal McGettigan. 1999.

19. *Hedge Funds: What Do We Really Know?* Barry Eichengreen and Donald Mathieson. 1999.

20. *Job Creation: Why Some Countries Do Better.* Pietro Garibaldi and Paolo Mauro. 2000.

21. *Improving Governance and Fighting Corruption in the Baltic and CIS Countries: The Role of the IMF.* Thomas Wolf and Emine Gürgen. 2000.

22. *The Challenge of Predicting Economic Crises.* Andrew Berg and Catherine Pattillo. 2000.

23. *Promoting Growth in Sub-Saharan Africa: Learning What Works.* Anupam Basu, Evangelos A. Calamitsis, and Dhaneshwar Ghura. 2000.

24. *Full Dollarization: The Pros and Cons.* Andrew Berg and Eduardo Borensztein. 2000.

25. *Controlling Pollution Using Taxes and Tradable Permits.* John Norregaard and Valérie Reppelin-Hill. 2000.

26. *Rural Poverty in Developing Countries: Implications for Public Policy.* Mahmood Hasan Khan. 2001.

27. *Tax Policy for Developing Countries.* Vito Tanzi and Howell Zee. 2001.

28. *Moral Hazard: Does IMF Financing Encourage Imprudence by Borrowers and Lenders?* Timothy Lane and Steven Phillips. 2002.